Cookbook with a lot of protein

High-protein, low-carb recipes that are easy to prepare at home!

Travis D. Richmond

Contents

Chapter One

Introduction

When it comes to your diet, protein is essential. Protein foods include all of the nutrients your body needs to be healthy and fit.. Your diet must consist mostly of eggs, fish, and meats. Meats such as beef, poultry, and fish are included in a low carb diet. Aside from meats such as lamb and pork, poultry such as turkey and prawns, crabs, salmon, and tuna are also high in protein. You may acquire protein from a variety of sources if you are a vegetarian. Some of these foods include butter, almonds, cheese, walnuts, eggs, peanuts, and tofu.

In order to consume meals that are rich in protein and low in carbohydrates, you should consume fruits and vegetables. The calorie and fat content of many veggies is very low. Corn, carrots, beets, peas, potatoes, parsnips, and squashes are examples of vegetables that should be avoided since they contain a significant quantity of carbohydrates. The fruits and vegetables limes, lemons, and barriers are also very beneficial to one's health. You should avoid dried fruits since they are heavy in sugar.

Make smart choices when it comes to carbohydrate items. Choose foods that are high in nutrients, such as brown rice, whole grain bread, and whole wheat pasta, among other things. In your diet, it will help to enhance the fiber. Sugary or refined carbs should be avoided in significant quantities. It is possible to gain weight by eating sweets, white bread, or cakes. Improve your diet by looking at the recipes listed below. The first chapter is titled "High Protein Low Carb Breakfast."

Breakfast recipes are provided here. Without any negative side effects, start your day with a high protein meal. Take a look at these dishes for breakfast and see how they work for you! Pumpkin Bread (Recipe #1)

This soft, moist, and swiftly baked pumpkin-flavored bread is a must-try for any pumpkin fanatic in your family.

Approximately 1 hour for preparation. 24 people may be served with this recipe.

3 quarts of sugar (approximate amount)

the oil from 1 cup of rapeseed egg whites (four)

Water in a 2/3 cup measuring cup

pumpkin puree (about 15 oz) ground ginger (about 2 teaspoons)

allspice berries (1 teaspoon)

ground cinnamon (about a teaspoon worth) cloves (ground) 1 teaspoon

approximately three and a half gallons flour that can be used for anything Baking soda, 2 teaspoons 1 1/2 teaspoons of sea salt

Baking powder (about 12 teaspoon)

Heat the oven to 350 degrees Fahrenheit for the following instructions. Prepare two loaf pans by greasing them with cooking spray.

Pour all of the ingredients into a mixing bowl. They should be blended together smoothly. Water should be added to make it smooth. Pour in the spices: ground cloves, ground cinnamon, ground cinnamon, and ginger.

Put all of the ingredients in a medium-sized mixing bowl and mix well. Now add the oil, and mix well again. Adding the dry ingredients to the pumpkin puree mixture will make it taste even better. All of the ingredients should be thoroughly combined. Using two pans, divide the mixture.

1 hour in the oven should suffice. A toothpick will enough for this verification process: If it comes out completely clean,

the bread is ready to be baked! Let's get this party started! Omelette with mushrooms and spinach (recipe no. 02)

If you have this for breakfast, it will make your day because it is simple to prepare, cheesy, and delicious, and it contains the goodness of spinach and mushrooms.

Approximately 30 minutes are required for preparation. 2 people may be served with this item. Ingredients:

8 ounces of egg replacement liquid is required.

Cheddar cheese, 1 tablespoon (or more), shredded 1/4 cup finely grated Parmesan cheese

Salt (14 tbsp.)

the following ingredients: 1/8 teaspoon of crushed black pepper, 1/8 teaspoon of garlic powder, 1/8 teaspoon of salt

red pepper flakes (about 1/8 teaspoon) the oil from one tablespoon of extra-virgin olive

chopped mushrooms (about 12 cup total)

1/2 cup minced onion, finely chopped

12 cup of spinach, chopped

Method: In a large mixing bowl, combine the parmesan and cheddar cheese, the egg, the red pepper flakes, the salt, the black pepper, and the garlic powder. Combine the ingredients in a large mixing bowl.

Preheat some oil in a non-stick pan over medium heat until it is hot but not smoking. Then sauté the mushrooms and onion for 4 – 5 minutes more. Take your time and let them get pliable.

It may be made even more delicious by using spinach. Cook for 3 – 4 minutes at a medium-high temperature. In a separate bowl, beat the eggs. Cook for at least 5-10 minutes longer than the recommended amount. Continue to wait until the egg has reached its mid-point.

For breakfast, you may cut it into wedges or eat it as-is. Enjoy. The Cheese Omelet (Recipe 03)

There is no doubt that this cheesy omelet will turn out to be something you will crave on weekends in order to make them even more enjoyable.

Duration of Preparation: 55 min 6 people may be accommodated. Ingredients:

Eggs (ten in number)

the milk in a third-cup measure

sodium chloride (12 tsp.)

Ingredients:

soy sauce (around 14 cup)

extra-firm tofu (eight ounces) (drained and cut into chunks) 1 zucchini cut into chunks.

Sesame oil (about 2 tablespoons)

onion, chopped (14 cup)

1 small red bell pepper chunk, finely diced jalapeno pepper, diced (optional)

A total of ten large mushrooms were used in this recipe.

peppercorns that have been ground to your specifications chilli garlic sauce (about 2 tablespoons) chili sauce (also known as sriracha).

Directions:

Toss together the tofu, zucchini, mushrooms, and red bell pepper in a large mixing bowl until evenly distributed. Put the sriracha sauce, pepper, sesame oil, onion, jalapeno, and soy sauce in a separate bowl and stir well. Combine the ingredients and stir well. Just a little toss will suffice. Put it in the refrigerator for one hour. Preheat the outdoor grill on a medium flame, with the grate greased and oiled.

Place tofu on skewers and secure with a rubber band. Grill them for a total of 10 minutes on both sides. Prepare dipping sauce to accompany the dish. Delicious Meat Recipes with a High Protein Content and Low Carbohydrate Content (Chapter 3).

This soft, moist, and swiftly baked pumpkin-flavored bread is a must-try for any pumpkin fanatic in your family.

Approximately 1 hour for preparation. 24 people may be served with this recipe.

3 quarts of sugar (approximate amount)

the oil from 1 cup of rapeseed egg whites (four)

Water in a 2/3 cup measuring cup

pumpkin puree (about 15 oz) ground ginger (about 2 teaspoons)

allspice berries (1 teaspoon)

ground cinnamon (about a teaspoon worth) cloves (ground) 1 teaspoon

approximately three and a half gallons flour that can be used for anything Baking soda, 2 teaspoons 1 1/2 teaspoons of sea salt

Baking powder (about 12 teaspoon)

Heat the oven to 350 degrees Fahrenheit for the following instructions. Prepare two loaf pans by greasing them with cooking spray.

Pour all of the ingredients into a mixing bowl. They should be blended together smoothly. Water should be added to make it smooth. Pour in the spices: ground cloves, ground cinnamon, ground cinnamon, and ginger.

Put all of the ingredients in a medium-sized mixing bowl and mix well. Now add the oil, and mix well again. Adding the dry ingredients to the pumpkin puree mixture will make it taste even better. All of the ingredients should be thoroughly combined. Using two pans, divide the mixture.

1 hour in the oven should suffice. A toothpick will enough for this verification process: If it comes out completely clean, the bread is ready to be baked! Let's get this party started! Omelette with mushrooms and spinach (recipe no. 02)

If you have this for breakfast, it will make your day because it is simple to prepare, cheesy, and delicious, and it contains the goodness of spinach and mushrooms.

Approximately 30 minutes are required for preparation. 2 people may be served with this item. Ingredients:

8 ounces of egg replacement liquid is required.

Cheddar cheese, 1 tablespoon (or more), shredded 1/4 cup finely grated Parmesan cheese

Salt (14 tbsp.)

the following ingredients: 1/8 teaspoon of crushed black pepper, 1/8 teaspoon of garlic powder, 1/8 teaspoon of salt red pepper flakes (about 1/8 teaspoon) the oil from one tablespoon of extra-virgin olive

chopped mushrooms (about 12 cup total)

1/2 cup minced onion, finely chopped

12 cup of spinach, chopped

Method: In a large mixing bowl, combine the parmesan and cheddar cheese, the egg, the red pepper flakes, the salt, the black pepper, and the garlic powder. Combine the ingredients in a large mixing bowl.

Preheat some oil in a non-stick pan over medium heat until it is hot but not smoking. Then sauté the mushrooms and onion for 4 – 5 minutes more. Take your time and let them get pliable.

It may be made even more delicious by using spinach. Cook for 3 – 4 minutes at a medium-high temperature. In a separate bowl, beat the eggs. Cook for at least 5-10 minutes longer than the recommended amount. Continue to wait until the egg has reached its mid-point.

For breakfast, you may cut it into wedges or eat it as-is. Enjoy. The Cheese Omelet (Recipe 03)

There is no doubt that this cheesy omelet will turn out to be something you will crave on weekends in order to make them even more enjoyable.

Duration of Preparation: 55 min 6 people may be accommodated. Ingredients:

Eggs (ten in number)

the milk in a third-cup measure

sodium chloride (12 tsp.)

Hot pepper sauce (about 4 dashes):

Cooked bacon (around 12 pounds) (chop into bite-size slices) 2 cups black olives, drained and pitted

14 cup of finely chopped green onions 2 plum tomatoes (chopped) Mushrooms, chopped into thirds of a cup

cheese shredded Colby-Monterey Jack (34 cup)

Heat the oven to 350 degrees Fahrenheit for the following instructions. Cooking spray should be used to grease a baking pan.

Add the milk and eggs to a mixing dish and stir well. Use an electric mixer to thoroughly mix them together. Season it with salt and pepper. On addition, you may use cheese, bacon, mushrooms, tomatoes, black olives, and green onions in your sandwich.

Place it on a baking sheet and bake it for 40-50 minutes, or until the eggs have settled down and become firm. For best results, cover the pan with a lid while baking. Breakfast Casserole (Recipe No. 04).

An excellent feature of the dish, though, is how versatile it is. Because it's so tasty and amazing, you'll want to prepare it every day.

Time required for preparation: 1 hour 15 minutes. 12 people may be accommodated by this recipe.

Ingredients:

1-pound of bacon, thinly cut. 1 sweet onion, finely chopped

frozen hash brown potatoes, shredded (four cups) (thawed) 9 softly whisked eggs, a light coating of flour,

cheese shredded (about 2 cups) Cheddar

1.5 cups cottage cheese (or ricotta) (small curd) 14 cups of Swiss cheese (one and a half pounds) (shredded)

Directions:

Preheat the oven to 350 degrees and butter a baking dish before beginning.

A medium flame should be used to heat a cast iron pan. Cook for 10 minutes with the bacon and onion. Toss them in a large mixing basin when they've finished cooking. Combine it with potatoes, Swiss cheese, cottage cheese, cheddar cheese, and eggs to make a delicious meal.. In a baking pan, place this.

40-50 minutes in the oven will be plenty to melt cheese and finish the cooking of the eggs. Cut the eggs into slices and place them on a serving plate or tray. A Peach Omelet (recipe 05).

This omelet will fill your home with an intoxicating scent as soon as it is prepared. Delicious and filling, it makes for an excellent breakfast.

Approximately 25 minutes are required for preparation. 3 people may be accommodated. Ingredients:

1 cup of peaches, peeled and sliced lemon juice (about 2 tbsp.)

Bacon (four slices) - Water (about 2 tablespoons) There are 6 eggs in this recipe.

1/4 cup chives, finely minced

Salt (14 tbsp.)

sugar (white): 1 tablespoon

powdered black pepper to taste (about 1/8 tsp. paprika (a pinch) is used in this recipe. Directions:

The peaches and lemon juice should be mixed together in a bowl. Using a big and deep saucepan, cook the bacon until crisp. Preheat the oven to 350°F (180°C). Draining and disintegrating it should be done after a while.

Combine the eggs, water, bacon, sugar, salt, chives, and black pepper in a large mixing bowl.

To finish, reheat the bacon in the same skillet. Place the egg mixture in the bowl and arrange the peach slices on top of the mixture. Cook it for about 1 minute over medium heat, covered.

Then take off the lid, boil the eggs, and you're ready to go! Paprika powder should be used. Allow for a few minutes of cooling time before serving. Vegetarian Recipes with a Lot of Protein (Chapter 2)

Recipes for vegetarians are included in this collection. The protein they provide will meet your requirements without putting on any extra pounds. Definitely worth a try and a taste. Tofu Bites (Recipe 06)

Those are the delectable tofu snacks that no one would want to miss out on at any price!

Approximately 25 minutes are required for preparation. 4 people may be accommodated by this recipe. Ingredients:

1 package of extra firm tofu (16 ounces)

soy sauce (around 14 cup)

maple syrup (about two tablespoons) ketchup (about 2 tablespoons)

the vinegar (about a tablespoon) 1-tablespoon cayenne pepper

Sesame seeds (1 tablespoon)

Garlic powder (1/4 teaspoon)

ground black pepper to taste (14 teaspoons)

the flavoring of liquid smoke 1 tsp

Pre-heat the oven to 375 degrees Fahrenheit for the following instructions: Grease the inside of a nonstick oven pan with olive oil. Slice the tofu into half-inch slices and press them to wring out any leftover water. Remove the cubes from the pan.

Pour the soy sauce, maple syrup, spicy sauce, vinegar, and ketchup into a mixing bowl and mix well. Sesame seeds, garlic powder, black pepper, and liquid smoke are also added to the mixture. Using a spatula, move the tofu cube around. Maintain a 5-minute period of relaxation.

Here are some delectable meat recipes. In terms of protein and carbohydrate content, they are excellent choices. Roasted Turkey (Recipe 11)

A robust flavor profile enables each and every flavor to blend beautifully, resulting in a turkey that is truly outstanding in taste.

Approximately 4 hours and 45 minutes were spent preparing this recipe. 16 people can be accommodated by this arrangement.

Ingredients:

olive oil (about a third of a cup)

seasoning (Italian seasoning, 1 tablespoon) minced garlic, 3 tablespoons (total)

ground black pepper (about a teaspoon) Depending on personal preference, salt

rosemary leaves, roughly chopped the whole turkey weighing 12 pounds chopped basil (about 1 tablespoon)

Directions:

Pre-heat the oven to 325 degrees F.

In a large mixing bowl, combine the olive oil, garlic, basil, Italian seasoning, salt, and black pepper; mix well to incorporate. Maintain a state of relaxation.

Now is the time to clean the turkey and trim away any excess fat. Remove the skin from the breasts by rubbing it together. Using your fingers, you can complete the task. Make a drumstick out of the skin instead of tearing it.

Apply rosemary to the leg, thigh, and skin at this point. A toothpick inserted into the meat of the breast will serve to seal the package.

Using 14 inch water, roast it. It should be roasted for 3-4 hours, until the temperature reaches 180 degrees Fahrenheit. A Roasted Pork Recipe (Recipe 12)

You can always serve it to your special guests because it has a mixed flavor that is slightly savory and sweet.

Approximately 3 hours and 20 minutes are required for preparation. The following ingredients are used to serve: 8 people

12-cup sugar (approximately)

1-tablespoon of sage leaves rubbed in Corn starch (about 1 tablespoon) is used in this recipe.

sodium chloride (12 tsp.)

Vinegar (1/4 cup)

peppercorns (14 tsp)

Water (about 14 cup)

1 crushed garlic clove (optional) Soy sauce (two tablespoons)

Boneless pork loin (about 5 pounds).

Directions:

Pre-heat the oven to 325 degrees F.

Sage, salt, pepper, and garlic are combined in a bowl. This should be served on top of pork. Place it in a roasting pan and roast it in the oven for about 30 minutes.

145 degrees Fahrenheit should be reached after 3 hours of baking.

While the sugar, soy sauce, water, cornstarch, and vinegar are heating in a pan, whisk together the remaining ingredients.

When bubbles begin to form in the pan, it is important to stir the mixture frequently to avoid burning. Hot food should be served. Meat Bulgogi (Recipe 13)

Known as FIRE MEAT, it is unquestionably the source of its extraordinary flavor and aroma, which is the reason for its other-worldly moniker.

Time required for preparation: 1 hour 15 minutes. 4 people may be accommodated by this recipe.

Ingredients:

Flap steak, pound, thinly sliced minced garlic (about 2 tablespoons)

sesame seeds (about a tablespoonful) soy sauce (about 5 tbsp.

Sesame oil (about 2 tablespoons)

White sugar (approximately 2 1/2 tablespoons)

12 teaspoons of freshly ground black pepper

green onion (about 14 cup) finely chopped

Preparation Instructions: Place the beef in a shallow dish and set aside. Now, combine the soy sauce, sugar, green onion, black pepper, sesame seeds, garlic, and sesame oil in a large mixing bowl and thoroughly combine the ingredients. Pour it over the beef and cover it with plastic wrap. Refrigerate for one hour and overnight.

Put the grill outside on high heat and let it get hot.

Grill the beef that has been marinated. Allow 1-2 minutes for each side to speak. Let's get this party started! BBQ Ribs (Recipe 14)

It is certain that your tender and juicy ribs will receive numerous compliments. Don't you think you should try it out today and eat some delicious ribs?

1 hour and 30 minutes for preparation 4 people may be accommodated by this recipe. Ingredients:

Salt (about 2 tablespoons)

Pork spare ribs (serves 2) (country style) barbecue sauce (one cup)

peppercorns (ground) to a tsp. Garlic powder (about 1 teaspoon)

Directions:

Pour water into a pot to cover the ribs by about an inch and a half or so. Now, add the garlic powder, black pepper, and salt to your taste preference and stir well. Keep an eye on the water as it comes to boil and the ribs as they soften. Pre-heat the oven to 325 degrees F.

Remove the ribs from the water pot and place them on a baking sheet to keep warm until dinner time. In this case, the dimensions should be 9x13 inches. After that, brush the ribs with the remaining barbecue sauce. It should be baked for one to one and a half hours after being covered with aluminum foil. Enjoy while it's still hot! Roasted Lamb (Recipe 15)

Not enough time to complete your project? It has arrived! When unexpected guests arrive, it is best for you to prepare as much as you can.

Time Required for Preparation: 40 min Approximately four people can be served. Ingredients:

8 skewers of rack of lamb that has been soaked and trim A half cup of breadcrumbs and a teaspoon of salt are combined.

minced garlic - 1 tbsp. black pepper (about 1 tsp.

chopped rosemary (about 2 tbsp.) olive oil (about 2 tablespoons)

3 Tablespoons of Dijon Mustard 1 teaspoon of salt 1 teaspoon of sugar tablespoon of extra-virgin olive oil 1 teaspoon black pepper 1 tablespoon extra-virgin olive oil

Preheating the oven to 450 degrees Fahrenheit is necessary. A mid-range oven rack should be used in a conventional oven.'

In a large mixing bowl, whisk together the pepper, salt, olive oil, bread crumbs, rosemary, and garlic. They should be thoroughly mixed together. It should be put aside for the time being.

Season the lamb rack with salt and pepper now. High heat should be applied to the olive oil in a heavy skillet at this point. Grill or sear the lamb for about 1-2 minutes on each side. Set it aside for a few minutes to cool. Take the mustard and rub it all over the rack of lamb. Put them in the bread crumbs after that to finish them off. Toss them in crumbs from all sides to coat them evenly. Place aluminum foil on the corners of the lamb rack bones to prevent charring.

Place the rack of lamb in a skillet and brown it on all sides, turning once. Roast it for 12-18 minutes, depending on how thick you like your slices of meat. It was completed in accordance with your preferences, such as rare, medium rare, and so on, Make necessary adjustments to the cooking time. Any sauce can be used to accompany it when served hot.

Delicious High Protein Snacks are covered in Chapter 4 of the book.

These delicious protein snacks have no negative impact on your diet or health because they are made from whole foods. Pour some tea on the side and enjoy your cookies! Here are some mouthwatering recipes to get you started. Enjoy. Filets de poisson (recipe number 16)

There is so much nutrition and flavor packed into these fillets, that you will undoubtedly enjoy them.

Time Required for Preparation: 20 min 2 people may be served with this item. Ingredients:

Fish (cod) weighing 4 oz (2 fillets)

To taste, season with pepper and salt to taste. depending on the need, 100 g of Greek Yogurt Cooking Spray or Vegetable oil

Pre-heat the oven to 350 degrees Fahrenheit before beginning.

Season fish fillets with salt and pepper. In a shallow baking dish, bake them for 15 minutes. Fillets of fish should be coated with yoghurt before serving.

Preheat the oven to 350°F and place the baking dish in the middle. Approximately 15 minutes should be sufficient to roast the fish fillets. Allow the yoghurt to cook until it turns a lighter shade of yellow. Sauce to taste can be added to the dish.

By covering the pan with a lid and cooking on the stove for 5 minutes, you can make it just as quickly.

Chickpea Salad (Recipe 17)

So why not make this salad a must-try because it contains an iconic blend of all of the flavors that have ever existed?

Time required for preparation: 1 hour and 5 minutes. The following ingredients are used to feed four people.

chickpeas or garbanzo beans (about 15 ounces) Cucumbers (one each) (finely chopped)

1 cup of grape tomatoes (halved) 14 cup of finely minced onions garlic cloves, minced (about 1 teaspoon) Parsley flakes (half a teaspoon)

dried basil, 14 teaspoons

parmesan cheese (about a tbsp (grated) 1 tablespoon of extra-virgin olive oil (optional)

vinegar (balsamic vinegar): 3 tablespoons

Salt (14 tbsp.)

Depending on your preference, add black pepper.

Directions:

Dry basil, parmesan cheese, onions, cucumbers, garlic, tomatoes, chickpeas, and parsley flakes are combined in a mixing bowl.

In a separate bowl, whisk together the olive oil, vinegar, pepper, and salt until well combined. Very carefully toss them.

Refrigerate the dish after you've added the seasonings to it. Allow 45 minutes for it to cool. Let's get this party started! Tortilla Chips (Recipe 18)

It is impossible to be disappointed with tortilla chips because they are crunchy and not overly greasy. You can whip them up in less than 30 minutes, which is a huge bonus.

Approximately 25 minutes are required for preparation. 6 people may be accommodated. Ingredients:

Tortillas de maiz de 12 ounces ground cumin (about 1 tsp.

chilli powder (one teaspoon) the salt (about 1 teaspoon).

1 cup freshly squeezed lime juice

vegetable oil (about 1 tbsp.)

Heat the oven to 350 degrees Fahrenheit for the following instructions.

Use a sharp knife to cut small wedges out of the tortillas, then set aside. On a greased baking sheet, arrange layers of tortillas. Toss it out of your mind!

Oil and lime juice should be combined. They should be thoroughly mixed together. Spraying tortillas will help to keep them moist longer.

Cumin, salt, and chili powder should be mixed together in a bowl. Place the tortilla chips on top of the mixture. Preheat the oven to 375°F and bake for 6-7 minutes. Using a rotational pan, you can make your chips crispier. Alternatively, you can serve it with salsa or any other sauce of your choosing. Zucchini Chips (Recipe 19)

All of the flavor that you could possibly want in a chip is in these tortillas. All that distinguishes them is that they contain a small amount of additional nutrition.

Approximately 30 minutes are required for preparation. 2 people may be served with this item. Ingredients:

Zucchini (approximately) 1 according to personal preference

olive oil with a garlic flavoring (about 2 tablespoons)

Pre-heat the oven to 375 degrees Fahrenheit for the following instructions:

Pour some ginger-infused olive oil into a bowl and top it with zucchini slices to serve. Very thoroughly combine and toss them Combining it with salt is the next step.

Place the zucchini slices on a baking sheet and bake for 20 minutes. Bake it in the preheated oven for 20 minutes at 350°F. Take a bite and enjoy it with the sauce of tomatoes. BBQ Meatballs (Recipe 20).

Your guests will rave about these delicious meatballs when you serve them at a special event! Put together these meatballs to earn the admiration and recognition that you deserve.

Total time required for preparation: 1 hour and 20 minutes. 8 people can be accommodated with this recipe.

pound of ground beef (as an ingredient).

sodium chloride (12 tsp.) 12 cups chopped onion, 2 eggs (or more)

12 cup of skim milk (or equivalent)

grilling sauce (about 18 ounces).

bread crumbs (approximately 1 1/2 cups).

Pre-heat the oven to 375 degrees Fahrenheit for the following instructions:

Using a large mixing bowl, combine the beef with the bread, the eggs with the onion, the salt, and the milk. Make meatballs in small, almost one-inch-diameter shapes to serve. The ball should be placed in a baking dish. 30 minutes in the oven should suffice. Toss meatballs with barbecue sauce. 30 minutes more in the oven should suffice. Take the hot spaghetti and place the balls on top of it. Serve immediately afterward. Cooking Low Carb Desserts with a High Protein Content (Chapter 5)

High protein dessert recipes are now available for you to try out. They are mouthwatering and delicious! Healthy dessert recipes are hard to come by, but these are some of the best around! In order to enjoy yourself while eating, Apple Cake (Recipe No.21)

Combine the eggs, water, bacon, sugar, salt, chives, and black pepper in a large mixing bowl.

To finish, reheat the bacon in the same skillet. Place the egg mixture in the bowl and arrange the peach slices on top of the mixture. Cook it for about 1 minute over medium heat, covered.

Then take off the lid, boil the eggs, and you're ready to go! Paprika powder should be used. Allow for a few minutes of cooling time before serving. Vegetarian Recipes with a Lot of Protein (Chapter 2)

Recipes for vegetarians are included in this collection. The protein they provide will meet your requirements without putting on any extra pounds. Definitely worth a try and a taste. Tofu Bites (Recipe 06)

Those are the delectable tofu snacks that no one would want to miss out on at any price!

Approximately 25 minutes are required for preparation. 4 people may be accommodated by this recipe. Ingredients:

1 package of extra firm tofu (16 ounces)

soy sauce (around 14 cup)

maple syrup (about two tablespoons) ketchup (about 2 tablespoons)

the vinegar (about a tablespoon) 1-tablespoon cayenne pepper

Sesame seeds (1 tablespoon)

Chapter Two

Garlic powder

(1/4 teaspoon)

ground black pepper to taste (14 teaspoons)

the flavoring of liquid smoke 1 tsp

Pre-heat the oven to 375 degrees Fahrenheit for the following instructions: Grease the inside of a nonstick oven pan with olive oil. Slice the tofu into half-inch slices and press them to wring out any leftover water. Remove the cubes from the pan.

Pour the soy sauce, maple syrup, spicy sauce, vinegar, and ketchup into a mixing bowl and mix well. Sesame seeds, garlic powder, black pepper, and liquid smoke are also added to the mixture. Using a spatula, move the tofu cube around. Maintain a 5-minute period of relaxation.

Here are some delectable meat recipes. In terms of protein and carbohydrate content, they are excellent choices. Roasted Turkey (Recipe 11)

A robust flavor profile enables each and every flavor to blend beautifully, resulting in a turkey that is truly outstanding in taste.

Approximately 4 hours and 45 minutes were spent preparing this recipe. 16 people can be accommodated by this arrangement.

Ingredients:

olive oil (about a third of a cup)

seasoning (Italian seasoning, 1 tablespoon) minced garlic, 3 tablespoons (total)

ground black pepper (about a teaspoon) Depending on personal preference, salt

rosemary leaves, roughly chopped the whole turkey weighing 12 pounds chopped basil (about 1 tablespoon)

Directions:

Pre-heat the oven to 325 degrees F.

In a large mixing bowl, combine the olive oil, garlic, basil, Italian seasoning, salt, and black pepper; mix well to incorporate. Maintain a state of relaxation.

Now is the time to clean the turkey and trim away any excess fat. Remove the skin from the breasts by rubbing it together. Using your fingers, you can complete the task. Make a drumstick out of the skin instead of tearing it.

Apply rosemary to the leg, thigh, and skin at this point. A toothpick inserted into the meat of the breast will serve to seal the package.

Using 14 inch water, roast it. It should be roasted for 3-4 hours, until the temperature reaches 180 degrees Fahrenheit. A Roasted Pork Recipe (Recipe 12)

You can always serve it to your special guests because it has a mixed flavor that is slightly savory and sweet.

Approximately 3 hours and 20 minutes are required for preparation. The following ingredients are used to serve: 8 people

12-cup sugar (approximately)

1-tablespoon of sage leaves rubbed in Corn starch (about 1 tablespoon) is used in this recipe.

sodium chloride (12 tsp.)

Vinegar (1/4 cup)

peppercorns (14 tsp)

Water (about 14 cup)

1 crushed garlic clove (optional) Soy sauce (two tablespoons)

Boneless pork loin (about 5 pounds).

Directions:

Pre-heat the oven to 325 degrees F.

Sage, salt, pepper, and garlic are combined in a bowl. This should be served on top of pork. Place it in a roasting pan and roast it in the oven for about 30 minutes.

145 degrees Fahrenheit should be reached after 3 hours of baking.

While the sugar, soy sauce, water, cornstarch, and vinegar are heating in a pan, whisk together the remaining ingredients. When bubbles begin to form in the pan, it is important to stir the mixture frequently to avoid burning. Hot food should be served. Meat Bulgogi (Recipe 13)

Known as FIRE MEAT, it is unquestionably the source of its extraordinary flavor and aroma, which is the reason for its other-worldly moniker.

Time required for preparation: 1 hour 15 minutes. 4 people may be accommodated by this recipe.

Ingredients:

Flap steak, pound, thinly sliced minced garlic (about 2 tablespoons)

sesame seeds (about a tablespoonful) soy sauce (about 5 tbsp.

Sesame oil (about 2 tablespoons)

White sugar (approximately 2 1/2 tablespoons)

12 teaspoons of freshly ground black pepper

green onion (about 14 cup) finely chopped

Preparation Instructions: Place the beef in a shallow dish and set aside. Now, combine the soy sauce, sugar, green onion, black pepper, sesame seeds, garlic, and sesame oil in a large mixing bowl and thoroughly combine the ingredients. Pour it over the beef and cover it with plastic wrap. Refrigerate for one hour and overnight.

Put the grill outside on high heat and let it get hot.

Grill the beef that has been marinated. Allow 1-2 minutes for each side to speak. Let's get this party started! BBQ Ribs (Recipe 14)

It is certain that your tender and juicy ribs will receive numerous compliments. Don't you think you should try it out today and eat some delicious ribs?

1 hour and 30 minutes for preparation 4 people may be accommodated by this recipe. Ingredients:

Salt (about 2 tablespoons)

Pork spare ribs (serves 2) (country style) barbecue sauce (one cup) peppercorns (ground) to a tsp. Garlic powder (about 1 teaspoon)

Directions:

Pour water into a pot to cover the ribs by about an inch and a half or so. Now, add the garlic powder, black pepper, and salt to your taste preference and stir well. Keep an eye on the water as it comes to boil and the ribs as they soften. Pre-heat the oven to 325 degrees F.

Your mouth will water at the delicious sweetness of this adorable apple cake. For those who enjoy cake, this would be at the top of their list.

Approximately 30 to 40 minutes are required for preparation. 12 people may be accommodated by this recipe.

Ingredients:

Baking powder (1 teaspoon) Baking soda, 1 teaspoon

sugar substitute (or brown sugar): 34 cup vanilla extract (about 2 teaspoons) 2 eggs

cinnamon (ground) 12 tbsp.

one-and-a-half teaspoons ground nutmeg

12-cup raisins (approximately).

sodium chloride (12 tsp.)

cups of unbleached white bread flour

unsweetened applesauce (approximately 1.5 cups)

Heat the oven to 350 degrees Fahrenheit for the following instructions. Nonstick cooking spray should be used to grease a pan. Allow it to be put to bed.

Using a large mixing bowl, sift together the flour, baking powder, nutmeg, baking soda, salt, and cinnamon. Similarly, set this aside.

The eggs should now be beaten. Using a mixer, combine the applesauce with the sugar and vanilla extract. In a separate bowl, whisk together the flour and salt. Make a smooth paste by thoroughly mixing the ingredients. Afterwards, mix in a handful of dried raisins.

Fill a greased loaf pan with this mixture. Preheat the oven to 350°F and bake for approximately 1 hour. Make use of a toothpick to see if it's done. This indicates that the cake is done when it comes out completely clean (clean). When the weather turns cold, take advantage of it. Sweet Bites (Recipe #22)

Many people will find the sweet bites to be an enlightening treat that they will find delicious.

Total time required for preparation: 2 hours and 20 minutes. 30 people can be accommodated by this recipe.

Ingredients:

The cream cheese should be 12 ounces total (whipped)
Wonderful Granular Salt (about 2 tablespoons)

Coffee, brewed to a 14-cup serving size

vanilla or chocolate extract (approximately 12 teaspoon) 1 cup whipped cream cheese

30 tart shells in miniature size Raspberry (approximately 30 berries).

Directions:

Combine coffee, vanilla, chocolate, splendid and cream cheese in a bowl. Combine them very well to make a smooth paste. Cover this mixture for 2 hours. If you want, you can put it into the\s

refrigerator as well.

Now, put it in a pastry bag with the help of a spoon and start filling the shells. Use raspberries for topping and serve and enjoy. Recipe 23: Sugar-free Pie

It is two in one in the case of this pie, no sugar, yet a lot of deliciousness. Perfect for you if you are trying to avoid sugar.

Preparation Time: 2 hours 10 minutes 8 people can be accommodated with this recipe.

Ingredients:

9 inches of cracker crust

1 ounce of sugar-free pudding (vanilla or chocolate flavour) (vanilla or chocolate flavour) 1 cup of cold milk

8 ounces of crushed pineapple 8 ounces whipped topping

1 cup of chopped pecans

Directions:\sMix pudding mix, milk in a medium mixing bowl. Combine whipped topping, pineapple and pecans. In a prepared crust, pour this mixture and let it for chilling for about 2 hours. Serve and chill. Recipe 24: Pumpkin Pie

We bet that you can never get over this very good-looking pumpkin pie that is wholesome. Try this tasty pie today!

Time required for preparation: 1 hour and 10 minutes.

Serves: 6 persons Ingredients:

pumpkin puree (about 15 oz)

½ cup of skim milk

1 tsp. of pie spice (pumpkin flavour) (pumpkin flavour) 8 ounces of fat-free whipped topping\sounce of sugar -free pudding mix (vanilla flavour) (vanilla flavour)

Directions:\sCombine pumpkin puree, pudding mix and milk in a bowl. Combine them very well. Mix pie spice with half whipped topping.

Place this mixture on a plate of pie. And add the rest of the topping on it. For about one hour, place it into the fridge. When chilled, serve it.

Cinnamon Cake (Recipe No.25)

Make it for your child's birthday or for any other special event, and it will be a hit. When making this delicious cake, the strong cinnamon taste is all that's needed.

Total time required for preparation: 1 hour and 30 minutes. 16 people may be accommodated with this arrangement.

Ingredients:

All-purpose flour is used to make cake cups.

Whole wheat pastry flour (about 12 cup). Sugar replacement (one-half cup)

brown sugar (half a cup)

Baking powder (between 1 and 14 teaspoons) ground cinnamon (about a teaspoon worth)

sodium chloride (12 tsp.)

Baking soda (half teaspoon)

milk (fat free) in a quarter-cup

Lightly beaten eggs (about 12 cups total) 1 / 3 cup apricots, chopped

canola oil (1/4 cup) - Vanilla Ganache (about 1 tablespoon)

chopped dark chocolate (about 3 ounces)

one-fourth cup cream of mushroom soup (fat-free)

Prepare the oven by preheating it to 325 degrees. Prepare a tube pan by greasing it. Lightly flour the pan to prevent sticking and releasing of the sauce. Restrain yourself from touching it.

In a large mixing basin, whisk together the brown sugar, baking powder, cinnamon, salt, baking soda, sugar replacement, and flour. They should be well combined.

Put all of the ingredients in another large mixing bowl and thoroughly mix them together. Now put all of the ingredients in a separate mixing bowl and thoroughly mix them together. Add the flour to the mixture at this point. In order to mix this mixture, you should use an electric mixer. For about 10 minutes, mix on medium speed. Fill a greased pan halfway with this mixture. Make sure the mixture is distributed evenly around the baking pan.

Dijon Mustard (about 1 tbsp. the honey (three tablespoons)

Put the grill outside on high heat and let it get hot.

Grill the beef that has been marinated. Allow 1-2 minutes for each side to speak. Let's get this party started! BBQ Ribs (Recipe 14)

It is certain that your tender and juicy ribs will receive numerous compliments. Don't you think you should try it out today and eat some delicious ribs?

1 hour and 30 minutes for preparation 4 people may be accommodated by this recipe. Ingredients:

Salt (about 2 tablespoons)

Pork spare ribs (serves 2) (country style) barbecue sauce (one cup)

peppercorns (ground) to a tsp. Garlic powder (about 1 teaspoon)

Directions:

Pour water into a pot to cover the ribs by about an inch and a half or so. Now, add the garlic powder, black pepper, and salt to your taste preference and stir well. Keep an eye on the water as it comes to boil and the ribs as they soften. Pre-heat the oven to 325 degrees F.

Your mouth will water at the delicious sweetness of this adorable apple cake. For those who enjoy cake, this would be at the top of their list.

Approximately 30 to 40 minutes are required for preparation. 12 people may be accommodated by this recipe.

Ingredients:

Baking powder (1 teaspoon) Baking soda, 1 teaspoon

sugar substitute (or brown sugar): 34 cup vanilla extract (about 2 teaspoons) 2 eggs

cinnamon (ground) 12 tbsp.

one-and-a-half teaspoons ground nutmeg

12-cup raisins (approximately).

sugar substitute (or brown sugar): 34 cup vanilla extract (about 2 teaspoons) 2 eggs

cinnamon (ground) 12 tbsp.

one-and-a-half teaspoons ground nutmeg

12-cup raisins (approximately).

sodium chloride (12 tsp.)

cups of unbleached white bread flour

unsweetened applesauce (approximately 1.5 cups)

Heat the oven to 350 degrees Fahrenheit for the following instructions. Nonstick cooking spray should be used to grease a pan. Allow it to be put to bed.

Using a large mixing bowl, sift together the flour, baking powder, nutmeg, baking soda, salt, and cinnamon. Similarly, set this aside.

The eggs should now be beaten. Using a mixer, combine the applesauce with the sugar and vanilla extract. In a separate bowl, whisk together the flour and salt. Make a smooth paste by thoroughly mixing the ingredients. Afterwards, mix in a handful of dried raisins.

Fill a greased loaf pan with this mixture. Preheat the oven to 350°F and bake for approximately 1 hour. Make use of a toothpick to see if it's done. This indicates that the cake is done when it comes out completely clean (clean). When the weather turns cold, take advantage of it. Sweet Bites (Recipe #22)

Many people will find the sweet bites to be an enlightening treat that they will find delicious.

Total time required for preparation: 2 hours and 20 minutes. 30 people can be accommodated by this recipe.

Ingredients:

The cream cheese should be 12 ounces total (whipped) Wonderful Granular Salt (about 2 tablespoons)

Coffee, brewed to a 14-cup serving size

vanilla or chocolate extract (approximately 12 teaspoon) 1 cup whipped cream cheese

30 tart shells in miniature size Raspberry (approximately 30 berries).

Directions:

Combine coffee, vanilla, chocolate, splendid and cream cheese in a bowl. Combine them very well to make a smooth paste. Cover this mixture for 2 hours. If you want, you can put it into the\s

refrigerator as well.

Now, put it in a pastry bag with the help of a spoon and start filling the shells. Use raspberries for topping and serve and enjoy. Recipe 23: Sugar-free Pie

It is two in one in the case of this pie, no sugar, yet a lot of deliciousness. Perfect for you if you are trying to avoid sugar.

Preparation Time: 2 hours 10 minutes 8 people can be accommodated with this recipe.

Bake it in the preheated oven for approximately 40-55 minutes. Check with a toothpick after 55 minutes to see whether it's done. This indicates that the cake is done when it comes out completely clean (clean). Leave it for a few minutes longer if it isn't ready yet. For approximately 10 minutes, place it on a cake stand to cool completely.

To make ganache, melt chocolate in a microwave-safe basin until it is smooth and creamy. Microwave it for about 1 minute on medium power, or until hot. Take a break for five minutes. Prepare a smooth paste by mixing all of the ingredients until smooth. Wait for it to thicken for a few minutes before serving. To finish the cake, pour over the chocolate mixture. When the dish is ready, serve it chilled. Healthful Appetizers for a High Protein Diet (Chapter 6)

Listed below are some absolutely fantastic appetizer recipes for your enjoyment. Using the recipes that follow you may create them that are very tasty, healthful, and simple to prepare. Definitely going to check these out soon. Pancakes (Recipe No. 26).

Considering that pancakes are sugary, they are also illuminating; thus, give them to your family and friends and you will get rave praises.

Time Required for Preparation: 20 min 8 people can be accommodated with this recipe. Ingredients:

All-purpose flour (about 1 and a half cups). milk (one and one-fourth cups).

Egg (a single one).

3 and a half teaspoons of baking powder, if desired the salt (about 1 teaspoon).

the butter (about three tablespoons) (melted) sugar (white): 1 tablespoon

Directions:

Put all of the ingredients in a large mixing basin and whisk until well combined. This is a fantastic combination of words! Pour egg, milk, and butter into a well in the center of the cake.

In a smooth mixture, thoroughly combine the ingredients. coat the pan with olive oil before you start cooking in it Set the heat to medium. Pour the pancake batter onto the heated pan and cook it for half a minute, or until the edges are golden. Permit both sides of the meat to get a dark brown color. Use your favorite syrup or sauce to accompany it. The recipe for Recipe 27 is a snack made using almonds and chicken.

There is nothing missing from this nutritious and unique cuisine. It has the most fantastic texture as well as an incredible appearance.

Duration of Preparation: 55 min The following ingredients are used to feed four people.

The chicken thigh weighs 500 grams (without skin and bones) 3 medium red onions (slices of red onion) (thick wedges)

1 red potato (500 g) (thick slices)

3 medium-sized red peppers, seeded but not cut into slices 1 garlic clove, peeled and minced

cumin, fennel seeds, and smoked paprika (1 tsp. each) in a small mortar and pestle the equivalent of three tablespoons Olive oil is a kind of oil that comes from the olive fruit.

1 lemon (including the zest and juice) Blanched almonds, roughly chopped (50 grams) Recipe includes 170g of Greek yogurt as an ingredient. Fresh parsley in a little handful

Directions:

Oven preheating at 400 degrees Fahrenheit Put everything in a big mixing bowl and mix well. Season the chicken with the seasonings and mix well.

Mix together the spices, lemon juice and garlic in a separate basin before adding the oil, olive oil, and lemon zest. Bake in two baking plates once you've spread the mixture over the potatoes and the chicken.

Roast it in the oven for 40 minutes, and then cook it for another 20 minutes. Additionally, add almonds.

In a separate dish, combine them with one tablespoon of minced parsley and yogurt.

Salmon and Soybean Soup (Recipe 28)

The combination of salmon and soybean will show to be well worth your effort since they provide the most delicious taste when cooked in conjunction with one another.

Approximately 25 minutes are required for preparation. 2 people may be served with this item. Ingredients:

Egg (a single one) (Omega-3)

Soybeans (200 g, defrosted 1 lemon juiced with 1 lemon's zest added oil (about 2 tablespoons) (Flaxseed)

Poultry lentils (Puy lentils): 250 grams

The spring onions are in a little cluster (sliced) 2 salmon fillets poached in butter (remove skin)

Directions:

Dijon Mustard (about 1 tbsp. the honey (three tablespoons)

Put the grill outside on high heat and let it get hot.

Grill the beef that has been marinated. Allow 1-2 minutes for each side to speak. Let's get this party started! BBQ Ribs (Recipe 14)

It is certain that your tender and juicy ribs will receive numerous compliments. Don't you think you should try it out today and eat some delicious ribs?

1 hour and 30 minutes for preparation 4 people may be accommodated by this recipe. Ingredients:

Salt (about 2 tablespoons)

Pork spare ribs (serves 2) (country style) barbecue sauce (one cup)

peppercorns (ground) to a tsp. Garlic powder (about 1 teaspoon)

Directions:

Pour water into a pot to cover the ribs by about an inch and a half or so. Now, add the garlic powder, black pepper, and salt to your taste preference and stir well. Keep an eye on the water as it comes to boil and the ribs as they soften. Pre-heat the oven to 325 degrees F.

Your mouth will water at the delicious sweetness of this adorable apple cake. For those who enjoy cake, this would be at the top of their list.

Approximately 30 to 40 minutes are required for preparation. 12 people may be accommodated by this recipe.

Ingredients:

Baking powder (1 teaspoon) Baking soda, 1 teaspoon

sugar substitute (or brown sugar): 34 cup vanilla extract (about 2 teaspoons) 2 eggs

cinnamon (ground) 12 tbsp.

one-and-a-half teaspoons ground nutmeg

12-cup raisins (approximately).

sugar substitute (or brown sugar): 34 cup vanilla extract (about 2 teaspoons) 2 eggs

cinnamon (ground) 12 tbsp.

one-and-a-half teaspoons ground nutmeg

12-cup raisins (approximately).

sodium chloride (12 tsp.)

cups of unbleached white bread flour

unsweetened applesauce (approximately 1.5 cups)

Heat the oven to 350 degrees Fahrenheit for the following instructions. Nonstick cooking spray should be used to grease a pan. Allow it to be put to bed.

Using a large mixing bowl, sift together the flour, baking powder, nutmeg, baking soda, salt, and cinnamon. Similarly, set this aside.

The eggs should now be beaten. Using a mixer, combine the applesauce with the sugar and vanilla extract. In a separate bowl, whisk together the flour and salt. Make a smooth paste by thoroughly mixing the ingredients. Afterwards, mix in a handful of dried raisins.

Fill a greased loaf pan with this mixture. Preheat the oven to 350°F and bake for approximately 1 hour. Make use of a toothpick to see if it's done. This indicates that the cake is done when it comes out completely clean (clean). When the weather turns cold, take advantage of it. Sweet Bites (Recipe #22)

Many people will find the sweet bites to be an enlightening treat that they will find delicious.

Total time required for preparation: 2 hours and 20 minutes. 30 people can be accommodated by this recipe.

Ingredients:

The cream cheese should be 12 ounces total (whipped) Wonderful Granular Salt (about 2 tablespoons)

Coffee, brewed to a 14-cup serving size

vanilla or chocolate extract (approximately 12 teaspoon) 1 cup whipped cream cheese

30 tart shells in miniature size Raspberry (approximately 30 berries).

Directions:

Combine coffee, vanilla, chocolate, splendid and cream cheese in a bowl. Combine them very well to make a smooth paste. Cover this mixture for 2 hours. If you want, you can put it into the\s

refrigerator as well.

Now, put it in a pastry bag with the help of a spoon and start filling the shells. Use raspberries for topping and serve and enjoy. Recipe 23: Sugar-free Pie

It is two in one in the case of this pie, no sugar, yet a lot of deliciousness. Perfect for you if you are trying to avoid sugar.

Preparation Time: 2 hours 10 minutes 8 people can be accommodated with this recipe.

Ingredients:

9 inches of cracker crust

1 ounce of sugar-free pudding (vanilla or chocolate flavour) (vanilla or chocolate flavour) 1 cup of cold milk

8 ounces of crushed pineapple 8 ounces whipped topping

1 cup of chopped pecans

Directions:\sMix pudding mix, milk in a medium mixing bowl. Combine whipped topping, pineapple and pecans. In a prepared crust, pour this mixture and let it for chilling for about 2 hours. Serve and chill. Recipe 24:

Pumpkin Pie

We bet that you can never get over this very good-looking pumpkin pie that is wholesome. Try this tasty pie today!

Time required for preparation: 1 hour and 10 minutes.

Serves: 6 persons Ingredients:

pumpkin puree (about 15 oz)

½ cup of skim milk

1 tsp. of pie spice (pumpkin flavour) (pumpkin flavour) 8 ounces of fat-free whipped topping\sounce of sugar -free pudding mix (vanilla flavour) (vanilla flavour)

Directions:\sCombine pumpkin puree, pudding mix and milk in a bowl. Combine them very well. Mix pie spice with half whipped topping.

Place this mixture on a plate of pie. And add the rest of the topping on it. For about one hour, place it into the fridge. When chilled, serve it.

Cinnamon Cake (Recipe No.25)

Make it for your child's birthday or for any other special event, and it will be a hit. When making this delicious cake, the strong cinnamon taste is all that's needed.

Total time required for preparation: 1 hour and 30 minutes. 16 people may be accommodated with this arrangement.

Ingredients:

All-purpose flour is used to make cake cups.

Whole wheat pastry flour (about 12 cup). Sugar replacement (one-half cup)

brown sugar (half a cup)

Baking powder (between 1 and 14 teaspoons) ground cinnamon (about a teaspoon worth)

sodium chloride (12 tsp.)

Baking soda (half teaspoon)

milk (fat free) in a quarter-cup

Lightly beaten eggs (about 12 cups total) 1 / 3 cup apricots, chopped

canola oil (1/4 cup) - Vanilla Ganache (about 1 tablespoon)

chopped dark chocolate (about 3 ounces)

one-fourth cup cream of mushroom soup (fat-free)

Prepare the oven by preheating it to 325 degrees. Prepare a tube pan by greasing it. Lightly flour the pan to prevent sticking and releasing of the sauce. Restrain yourself from touching it.

In a large mixing basin, whisk together the brown sugar, baking powder, cinnamon, salt, baking soda, sugar replacement, and flour. They should be well combined.

Put all of the ingredients in another large mixing bowl and thoroughly mix them together. Now put all of the ingredients in a separate mixing bowl and thoroughly mix them together. Add the flour to the mixture at this point. In order to mix this mixture, you should use an electric mixer. For about 10 minutes, mix on medium speed. Fill a greased pan halfway with this mixture. Make sure the mixture is distributed evenly around the baking pan.

Bake it in the preheated oven for approximately 40-55 minutes. Check with a toothpick after 55 minutes to see whether it's done. This indicates that the cake is done when it comes out completely clean (clean). Leave it for a few minutes longer if it isn't ready yet. For approximately 10 minutes, place it on a cake stand to cool completely.

To make ganache, melt chocolate in a microwave-safe basin until it is smooth and creamy. Microwave it for about 1 minute on medium power, or until hot. Take a break for five minutes. Prepare a smooth paste by mixing all of the ingredients until smooth. Wait for it to thicken for a few minutes before serving. To finish the cake, pour over the chocolate mixture. When the dish is ready, serve it chilled. Healthful Appetizers for a High Protein Diet (Chapter 6)

Listed below are some absolutely fantastic appetizer recipes for your enjoyment. Using the recipes that follow you may create them that are very tasty, healthful, and simple to prepare. Definitely going to check these out soon. Pancakes (Recipe No. 26).

Considering that pancakes are sugary, they are also illuminating; thus, give them to your family and friends and you will get rave praises.

Time Required for Preparation: 20 min 8 people can be accommodated with this recipe. Ingredients:

All-purpose flour (about 1 and a half cups). milk (one and one-fourth cups).

Egg (a single one).

3 and a half teaspoons of baking powder, if desired the salt (about 1 teaspoon).

the butter (about three tablespoons) (melted) sugar (white): 1 tablespoon

Directions:

Put all of the ingredients in a large mixing basin and whisk until well combined. This is a fantastic combination of words! Pour egg, milk, and butter into a well in the center of the cake.

In a smooth mixture, thoroughly combine the ingredients. coat the pan with olive oil before you start cooking in it Set the heat to medium. Pour the pancake batter onto the heated pan and cook it for half a minute, or until the edges are golden. Permit both sides of the meat to get a dark brown color. Use your favorite syrup or sauce to accompany it. The recipe for Recipe 27 is a snack made using almonds and chicken.

There is nothing missing from this nutritious and unique cuisine. It has the most fantastic texture as well as an incredible appearance.

Duration of Preparation: 55 min The following ingredients are used to feed four people.

The chicken thigh weighs 500 grams (without skin and bones) 3 medium red onions (slices of red onion) (thick wedges)

1 red potato (500 g) (thick slices)

3 medium-sized red peppers, seeded but not cut into slices 1 garlic clove, peeled and minced

cumin, fennel seeds, and smoked paprika (1 tsp. each) in a small mortar and pestle the equivalent of three tablespoons Olive oil is a kind of oil that comes from the olive fruit.

1 lemon (including the zest and juice) Blanched almonds, roughly chopped (50 grams) Recipe includes 170g of Greek yogurt as an ingredient. Fresh parsley in a little handful

Directions:

Oven preheating at 400 degrees Fahrenheit Put everything in a big mixing bowl and mix well. Season the chicken with the seasonings and mix well.

Mix together the spices, lemon juice and garlic in a separate basin before adding the oil, olive oil, and lemon zest. Bake in two baking plates once you've spread the mixture over the potatoes and the chicken.

Roast it in the oven for 40 minutes, and then cook it for another 20 minutes. Additionally, add almonds.

In a separate dish, combine them with one tablespoon of minced parsley and yogurt.

Directions:

Fry the onion for around 4 minutes in 2 tablespoons of olive oil. Maintain a low temperature. Now, combine the mustard and honey in a small bowl and set it aside until you need it.

Take a bowl and put it in your hands. Make four patties for a burger by combining all of the burger ingredients together. Put one tablespoon of olive oil in a skillet and fry the burger patties until they are browned on both sides, about five minutes. Cook them for 10-12 minutes, depending on their size. Honey and mustard sauce may be served on the side with any bread or bun of your choosing.

Burger patties may also be topped with a variety of ingredients such as mushrooms, honey mustard, tomato, sautéed tomato, and romaine lettuce.

sodium chloride (12 tsp.)

cups of unbleached white bread flour

unsweetened applesauce (approximately 1.5 cups)

Heat the oven to 350 degrees Fahrenheit for the following instructions. Nonstick cooking spray should be used to grease a pan. Allow it to be put to bed.

Using a large mixing bowl, sift together the flour, baking powder, nutmeg, baking soda, salt, and cinnamon. Similarly, set this aside.

The eggs should now be beaten. Using a mixer, combine the applesauce with the sugar and vanilla extract. In a separate bowl, whisk together the flour and salt. Make a smooth paste by thoroughly mixing the ingredients. Afterwards, mix in a handful of dried raisins.

Fill a greased loaf pan with this mixture. Preheat the oven to 350°F and bake for approximately 1 hour. Make use of a toothpick to see if it's done. This indicates that the cake is done when it comes out completely clean (clean). When the weather turns cold, take advantage of it. Sweet Bites (Recipe #22)

Many people will find the sweet bites to be an enlightening treat that they will find delicious.

Total time required for preparation: 2 hours and 20 minutes. 30 people can be accommodated by this recipe.

Ingredients:

The cream cheese should be 12 ounces total (whipped) Wonderful Granular Salt (about 2 tablespoons)

Coffee, brewed to a 14-cup serving size

vanilla or chocolate extract (approximately 12 teaspoon) 1 cup whipped cream cheese

30 tart shells in miniature size Raspberry (approximately 30 berries).

Directions:

Combine coffee, vanilla, chocolate, splendid and cream cheese in a bowl. Combine them very well to make a smooth paste.

Cover this mixture for 2 hours. If you want, you can put it into the\s

refrigerator as well.

Now, put it in a pastry bag with the help of a spoon and start filling the shells. Use raspberries for topping and serve and enjoy. Recipe 23: Sugar-free Pie

It is two in one in the case of this pie, no sugar, yet a lot of deliciousness. Perfect for you if you are trying to avoid sugar.

Preparation Time: 2 hours 10 minutes 8 people can be accommodated with this recipe.

Ingredients:

9 inches of cracker crust

1 ounce of sugar-free pudding (vanilla or chocolate flavour) (vanilla or chocolate flavour) 1 cup of cold milk

8 ounces of crushed pineapple 8 ounces whipped topping

1 cup of chopped pecans

Directions:\sMix pudding mix, milk in a medium mixing bowl. Combine whipped topping, pineapple and pecans. In a prepared crust, pour this mixture and let it for chilling for about 2 hours. Serve and chill. Recipe 24: Pumpkin Pie

We bet that you can never get over this very good-looking pumpkin pie that is wholesome. Try this tasty pie today!

Time required for preparation: 1 hour and 10 minutes.

Serves: 6 persons Ingredients:

pumpkin puree (about 15 oz)

½ cup of skim milk

1 tsp. of pie spice (pumpkin flavour) (pumpkin flavour) 8 ounces of fat-free whipped topping\sounce of sugar -free pudding mix (vanilla flavour) (vanilla flavour)

Directions:\sCombine pumpkin puree, pudding mix and milk in a bowl. Combine them very well. Mix pie spice with half whipped topping.

Place this mixture on a plate of pie. And add the rest of the topping on it. For about one hour, place it into the fridge. When chilled, serve it.

Chapter Four

Hot pepper sauce

(about 4 dashes):

Cooked bacon (around 12 pounds) (chop into bite-size slices)
2 cups black olives, drained and pitted

14 cup of finely chopped green onions 2 plum tomatoes
(chopped) Mushrooms, chopped into thirds of a cup

cheese shredded Colby-Monterey Jack (34 cup)

Heat the oven to 350 degrees Fahrenheit for the following
instructions. Cooking spray should be used to grease a baking
pan.

Add the milk and eggs to a mixing dish and stir well. Use an
electric mixer to thoroughly mix them together. Season it with
salt and pepper. On addition, you may use cheese, bacon,
mushrooms, tomatoes, black olives, and green onions in your
sandwich.

Place it on a baking sheet and bake it for 40-50 minutes, or until the eggs have settled down and become firm. For best results, cover the pan with a lid while baking. Breakfast Casserole (Recipe No. 04).

An excellent feature of the dish, though, is how versatile it is. Because it's so tasty and amazing, you'll want to prepare it every day.

Time required for preparation: 1 hour 15 minutes. 12 people may be accommodated by this recipe.

Ingredients:

1-pound of bacon, thinly cut. 1 sweet onion, finely chopped

frozen hash brown potatoes, shredded (four cups) (thawed) 9 softly whisked eggs, a light coating of flour,

cheese shredded (about 2 cups) Cheddar

1.5 cups cottage cheese (or ricotta) (small curd) 14 cups of Swiss cheese (one and a half pounds) (shredded)

Directions:

Preheat the oven to 350 degrees and butter a baking dish before beginning.

A medium flame should be used to heat a cast iron pan. Cook for 10 minutes with the bacon and onion. Toss them in a large mixing basin when they've finished cooking. Combine it with potatoes, Swiss cheese, cottage cheese, cheddar cheese, and eggs to make a delicious meal.. In a baking pan, place this.

40-50 minutes in the oven will be plenty to melt cheese and finish the cooking of the eggs. Cut the eggs into slices and place them on a serving plate or tray. A Peach Omelet (recipe 05).

This omelet will fill your home with an intoxicating scent as soon as it is prepared. Delicious and filling, it makes for an excellent breakfast.

Approximately 25 minutes are required for preparation. 3 people may be accommodated. Ingredients:

1 cup of peaches, peeled and sliced lemon juice (about 2 tbsp.)

Bacon (four slices) - Water (about 2 tablespoons) There are 6 eggs in this recipe.

1/4 cup chives, finely minced

Salt (14 tbsp.)

sugar (white): 1 tablespoon

powdered black pepper to taste (about 1/8 tsp. paprika (a pinch) is used in this recipe. Directions:

The peaches and lemon juice should be mixed together in a bowl. Using a big and deep saucepan, cook the bacon until crisp. Preheat the oven to 350°F (180°C). Draining and disintegrating it should be done after a while.

Combine the eggs, water, bacon, sugar, salt, chives, and black pepper in a large mixing bowl.

To finish, reheat the bacon in the same skillet. Place the egg mixture in the bowl and arrange the peach slices on top of the mixture. Cook it for about 1 minute over medium heat, covered.

Then take off the lid, boil the eggs, and you're ready to go! Paprika powder should be used. Allow for a few minutes of cooling time before serving. Vegetarian Recipes with a Lot of Protein (Chapter 2)

Recipes for vegetarians are included in this collection. The protein they provide will meet your requirements without putting on any extra pounds. Definitely worth a try and a taste. Tofu Bites (Recipe 06)

Those are the delectable tofu snacks that no one would want to miss out on at any price!

Approximately 25 minutes are required for preparation. 4 people may be accommodated by this recipe. Ingredients:

1 package of extra firm tofu (16 ounces)

soy sauce (around 14 cup)

maple syrup (about two tablespoons) ketchup (about 2 tablespoons) the vinegar (about a tablespoon) 1-tablespoon cayenne pepper

Sesame seeds (1 tablespoon)

Garlic powder (1/4 teaspoon)

ground black pepper to taste (14 teaspoons)

the flavoring of liquid smoke 1 tsp

Pre-heat the oven to 375 degrees Fahrenheit for the following instructions: Grease the inside of a nonstick oven pan with olive oil. Slice the tofu into half-inch slices and press them to wring out any leftover water. Remove the cubes from the pan.

Pour the soy sauce, maple syrup, spicy sauce, vinegar, and ketchup into a mixing bowl and mix well. Sesame seeds, garlic powder, black pepper, and liquid smoke are also added to the mixture. Using a spatula, move the tofu cube around. Maintain a 5-minute period of relaxation.

After that, spread them out on a baking sheet to cool. 15 minutes is sufficient time to bake them. Wait until they get a dark brown color before eating them. Let's get this party started! The seventh recipe is Lasagna made using tofu.

As a result of its wonderful taste and fragrance, this lasagna is ideal for feeding to distinguished visitors.

Duration of Preparation: 55 min The following ingredients are used to prepare this dish for 7 people.

lasagna noodles (around 6 ounces) (uncooked) a dozen ounces of firm tofu crumbled

egg whites (a total of 2)

Salt (14 tbsp.)

black pepper (14 tsp.)

14.4 tsp. nutmeg (ground) 1 cup of spaghetti sauce, 2 tablespoons of milk dried parsley (about 1 tbsp.

6 cups (or more) of grated mozzarella cheese (divided)

Parmesan cheese, grated (12 cup), for garnish

Heat the oven to 350 degrees Fahrenheit for the following instructions.

Toss lasagna in a pot of boiling water. Continue to boil for another 8-10 minutes until the water is completely dissolved. Empty it out completely!

To make the scrambled eggs, combine them in a large mixing bowl with the cheeses and salt. Add the parsley and pepper to taste. In a baking dish, arrange one layer.

Start with a layer of lasagna noodles and a layer of sauce mix, then continue this layering process with more sauce. Extra parmesan and mozzarella cheese may be sprinkled on top if you have any left over!

25-35 minutes in the oven and it's ready to serve! Enjoy. Vegetarian Chili (Recipe No. 08).

This spicy, delectable vegetarian chili is jam-packed with beans, veggies, and spice to satisfy any need.

Time required for preparation: 1 hour and 10 minutes. 6 people may be accommodated.

Ingredients:

5 onions, finely chopped

Burger-style crumbles (around 12 ounces) chilli powder (about 3 tablespoons), to taste

beans (black) weighing 30 ounces (drained and rinsed) Cumin (ground): 1 and a half tablespoons

Beans in their natural state, about 30 ounces (dark) Garlic powder (about 1 teaspoon)

beans (red kidney beans) weighing about 15 ounces (light) 2 bay leaves (1 tablespoon)

chopped tomatoes (total of 29 ounces) Tomato juice (about 12 oz.)

To taste, season with pepper and salt

Method: In a large pot, combine the onions, tomato juice, chili powder, tomatoe puree, cumin, pepper, garlic powder, salt, black beans, burger-style crumbles, bay leaves, and kidney beans. Bring to a boil, then reduce the heat to low and simmer for 30 minutes.

They should be combined properly. Allow 1 hour of cooking time at a low temperature to complete the recipe Hot food should be served. Cooking with Bell Peppers (Recipe 09)

There's something about this sweet, mild-flavored bell pepper with an iconic flavor that you won't want to miss out on!

Time required for preparation: 1 hour and 10 minutes. 4 people may be accommodated by this recipe.

Ingredients:

parsley (about 2 tablespoons)

12 cup of white rice (or other grain of choice) (uncooked) 2 quarts of tomato sauce (or whatever you prefer)

a quarter-cup of liquid

the mozzarella cheese (about four ounces) (shredded) peppers (green): 4 oz.

Season with salt to suit personal preference. 1 small onion, finely chopped

peppercorns, freshly ground to your liking olive oil (about 4 tbsp.) vegetable protein (eight ounces) (textured)

Using a pan, combine the rice with water until it is fully cooked (see directions above). Allow 15 minutes on a low heat setting. Pre-heat the oven to 400 degrees Fahrenheit.

Using a sharp knife, cut the tops off of the bell pepper and discard the seeds. In a baking dish, arrange them.

Heat the oil in a saucepan. The onions and peppers should be sautéed together. Wait for them to become pliable before proceeding. In a separate bowl, combine the vegetable protein powder and parsley. Preheat the oven to 200°F and cook for 5 minutes. Then add the tomato sauce and mix it all together.

Season to your liking with salt and pepper. Fill peppers with this mixture, and top each pepper with a tomato and tomato sauce (if using). 40 to 45 minutes in the oven should suffice. Now, sprinkle on the mozzarella cheese and bake until it is completely melted and bubbly. Enjoy while still warm. Grilled Tofu (Recipe 10)

This dish is a must-try because it absorbs all of the flavors from the grill. It's free today, so give it a shot!

Duration of preparation: 1 hour and twenty-five minutes 2 people may be served with this item.

Chapter Five

Cinnamon Cake

Recipe No.25)

Make it for your child's birthday or for any other special event, and it will be a hit. When making this delicious cake, the strong cinnamon taste is all that's needed.

Total time required for preparation: 1 hour and 30 minutes. 16 people may be accommodated with this arrangement.

Ingredients:

All-purpose flour is used to make cake cups.

Whole wheat pastry flour (about 12 cup). Sugar replacement (one-half cup)

brown sugar (half a cup)

Baking powder (between 1 and 14 teaspoons) ground cinnamon (about a teaspoon worth)

Prepare a pan by filling it halfway with cold water and cracking an egg into it; set this aside. On a medium burner, bring it to a boil for around 4-8 minutes, covered. Combine it with soy beans at the last minute to save time. Afterward, drain it for 8 minutes. After a few seconds of running water, remove them from the water source. Removing the shells from the eggs is a good idea. The eggs should be cut into wedges of six pieces each. Beans and eggs should be kept at a separate location.

Assemble the ingredients in a large mixing bowl, mixing thoroughly after each addition of lemon juice and lemon zest. Soybeans, onions, and lentils should all be combined.

Placing the salmon on top of the mixture in two bowls or plates is a nice touch. Alternatively, brown bread may be used to serve it.

Chicken Skewers (Recipe 29).

Make a single serving for your family and watch them return time and time again for the chicken skewers you've prepared.

Time Required for Preparation: 50 min 8 people may be accommodated with this recipe. Ingredients:

potatoes (500 g) that are brand fresh

1 cup chopped mint, chives, and parsley, 3 tablespoons (each) Olive oil (about 6 tbsp.):

lemon juice (about 2 tbsp.)

the chicken breasts (500 g total) (without skin and 3cm chunks)
1 red onion that has been peeled

remove seeds and cut into 3cm pieces from 1 red pepper
lemon Relish (eight wedges) 1 Ingredients tomatoes in full
ripeness

2 green chillies (seedless and chopped) minced garlic (about 2
cloves)

olive oil (about 4 tbsp.)

vinegar (white) (around a tablespoon)

It is necessary to soak wooden or bamboo pots in cold water
before cooking if the dish is to be served that way. Continue
to immerse them in water for about 30 minutes.

Boil potatoes in salted water for 10-12 minutes until they are
soft. Then drain them after they have boiled. Set them aside
for a few minutes to allow them to cool completely.

Put all of the ingredients in a mixing bowl except the oil and
pepper. Now, combine the chicken and potatoes with the
lemon mixture.

Everything should be well combined and combined. Onions
should be sliced into six wedges, with the layers of each wedge
being separated. Pepper and onion should now be mixed
together. They should be well mixed together.

Making Relish: To make relish, cut tomatoes in half and discard the seeds. Tomatoes should be chopped fine. Combine the garlic, oil, tomatoes, pepper, salt, and chilies in a large mixing bowl until well combined. Place the mixture in a serving dish. a.

Put the chicken, pepper, onion, and potatoes on eight skewers and grill them until they are cooked through. Put a lemon wedge on each skewer and pierce it through the middle.

In the oven or on a barbecue, cook for about 5-6 minutes on each side over a medium flame for about 5-6 minutes total. Tomato relish should be served alongside. Lentil Sandwich (Recipe no. 30)

In situations when you need to eat something quickly, this sandwich is the finest alternative.

Approximately 30 minutes are required for preparation. 4 people may be accommodated by this recipe. Ingredients:

olive oil (about a tbsp.)

red onion, diced (about 14 cup)

Cooked Quinoa (about 1 cup) (make according to the instructions of package) one-and-a-half cups of brown lentils, rinsed and cooked

3 to 4 ounces of finely chopped green peppers roll oats (about 1/3 cup)

Whole-wheat pastry flour (14 cup) cornstarch (about 2 tablespoons).

14 cup bread crumbs made from whole wheat

Garlic powder (1/4 teaspoon)

12 tsp. cumin (or equivalent)

tsp. paprika (optional).

To taste, season with pepper and salt

Ingredients of Honey Mustard

Dijon Mustard (about 1 tbsp. the honey (three tablespoons)

Put the grill outside on high heat and let it get hot.

Grill the beef that has been marinated. Allow 1-2 minutes for each side to speak. Let's get this party started! BBQ Ribs (Recipe 14)

It is certain that your tender and juicy ribs will receive numerous compliments. Don't you think you should try it out today and eat some delicious ribs?

1 hour and 30 minutes for preparation 4 people may be accommodated by this recipe. Ingredients:

Salt (about 2 tablespoons)

Pork spare ribs (serves 2) (country style) barbecue sauce (one cup) peppercorns (ground) to a tsp. Garlic powder (about 1 teaspoon)

Directions:

Pour water into a pot to cover the ribs by about an inch and a half or so. Now, add the garlic powder, black pepper, and salt to your taste preference and stir well. Keep an eye on the water as it comes to boil and the ribs as they soften. Pre-heat the oven to 325 degrees F.

Your mouth will water at the delicious sweetness of this adorable apple cake. For those who enjoy cake, this would be at the top of their list.

Approximately 30 to 40 minutes are required for preparation. 12 people may be accommodated by this recipe.

Ingredients:

Baking powder (1 teaspoon) Baking soda, 1 teaspoon

sugar substitute (or brown sugar): 34 cup vanilla extract (about 2 teaspoons) 2 eggs

cinnamon (ground) 12 tbsp.

one-and-a-half teaspoons ground nutmeg

12-cup raisins (approximately).

sodium chloride (12 tsp.)

cups of unbleached white bread flour

unsweetened applesauce (approximately 1.5 cups)

Heat the oven to 350 degrees Fahrenheit for the following instructions. Nonstick cooking spray should be used to grease a pan. Allow it to be put to bed.

Using a large mixing bowl, sift together the flour, baking powder, nutmeg, baking soda, salt, and cinnamon. Similarly, set this aside.

The eggs should now be beaten. Using a mixer, combine the applesauce with the sugar and vanilla extract. In a separate bowl, whisk together the flour and salt. Make a smooth paste by thoroughly mixing the ingredients. Afterwards, mix in a handful of dried raisins.

Fill a greased loaf pan with this mixture. Preheat the oven to 350°F and bake for approximately 1 hour. Make use of a toothpick to see if it's done. This indicates that the cake is done when it comes out completely clean (clean). When the weather turns cold, take advantage of it. Sweet Bites (Recipe #22)

Many people will find the sweet bites to be an enlightening treat that they will find delicious.

Total time required for preparation: 2 hours and 20 minutes. 30 people can be accommodated by this recipe.

Ingredients:

The cream cheese should be 12 ounces total (whipped)
Wonderful Granular Salt (about 2 tablespoons)

Coffee, brewed to a 14-cup serving size

vanilla or chocolate extract (approximately 12 teaspoon) 1 cup whipped cream cheese

30 tart shells in miniature size Raspberry (approximately 30 berries).

Directions:

Combine coffee, vanilla, chocolate, splendid and cream cheese in a bowl. Combine them very well to make a smooth paste. Cover this mixture for 2 hours. If you want, you can put it into the\s

refrigerator as well.

Now, put it in a pastry bag with the help of a spoon and start filling the shells. Use raspberries for topping and serve and enjoy. Recipe 23: Sugar-free Pie

It is two in one in the case of this pie, no sugar, yet a lot of deliciousness. Perfect for you if you are trying to avoid sugar.

Preparation Time: 2 hours 10 minutes 8 people can be accommodated with this recipe.

Ingredients:

9 inches of cracker crust

1 ounce of sugar-free pudding (vanilla or chocolate flavour) (vanilla or chocolate flavour) 1 cup of cold milk

8 ounces of crushed pineapple 8 ounces whipped topping

1 cup of chopped pecans

Directions:\sMix pudding mix, milk in a medium mixing bowl. Combine whipped topping, pineapple and pecans. In a prepared crust, pour this mixture and let it for chilling for about 2 hours. Serve and chill. Recipe 24: Pumpkin Pie

We bet that you can never get over this very good-looking pumpkin pie that is wholesome. Try this tasty pie today!

Time required for preparation: 1 hour and 10 minutes.

Serves: 6 persons Ingredients:

pumpkin puree (about 15 oz)

½ cup of skim milk

1 tsp. of pie spice (pumpkin flavour) (pumpkin flavour) 8 ounces of fat-free whipped topping\sounce of sugar -free pudding mix (vanilla flavour) (vanilla flavour)

Directions:\sCombine pumpkin puree, pudding mix and milk in a bowl. Combine them very well. Mix pie spice with half whipped topping.

Place this mixture on a plate of pie. And add the rest of the topping on it. For about one hour, place it into the fridge. When chilled, serve it.

Cinnamon Cake (Recipe No.25)

Make it for your child's birthday or for any other special event, and it will be a hit. When making this delicious cake, the strong cinnamon taste is all that's needed.

Total time required for preparation: 1 hour and 30 minutes. 16 people may be accommodated with this arrangement.

Ingredients:

All-purpose flour is used to make cake cups.

Whole wheat pastry flour (about 12 cup). Sugar replacement (one-half cup)

brown sugar (half a cup)

Baking powder (between 1 and 14 teaspoons) ground cinnamon (about a teaspoon worth)

sodium chloride (12 tsp.)

Baking soda (half teaspoon)

milk (fat free) in a quarter-cup

Lightly beaten eggs (about 12 cups total) 1 / 3 cup apricots, chopped

canola oil (1/4 cup) - Vanilla Ganache (about 1 tablespoon)

chopped dark chocolate (about 3 ounces)

one-fourth cup cream of mushroom soup (fat-free)

Prepare the oven by preheating it to 325 degrees. Prepare a tube pan by greasing it. Lightly flour the pan to prevent sticking and releasing of the sauce. Restrain yourself from touching it.

In a large mixing basin, whisk together the brown sugar, baking powder, cinnamon, salt, baking soda, sugar replacement, and flour. They should be well combined.

Put all of the ingredients in another large mixing bowl and thoroughly mix them together. Now put all of the ingredients in a separate mixing bowl and thoroughly mix them together. Add the flour to the mixture at this point. In order to mix this mixture, you should use an electric mixer. For about 10 minutes, mix on medium speed. Fill a greased pan halfway with this mixture. Make sure the mixture is distributed evenly around the baking pan.

Bake it in the preheated oven for approximately 40-55 minutes. Check with a toothpick after 55 minutes to see whether it's done. This indicates that the cake is done when it comes out completely clean (clean). Leave it for a few minutes longer if it isn't ready yet. For approximately 10 minutes, place it on a cake stand to cool completely.

To make ganache, melt chocolate in a microwave-safe basin until it is smooth and creamy. Microwave it for about 1 minute on medium power, or until hot. Take a break for five minutes. Prepare a smooth paste by mixing all of the ingredients until smooth. Wait for it to thicken for a few minutes before serving. To finish the cake, pour over the chocolate mixture. When the dish is ready, serve it chilled. Healthful Appetizers for a High Protein Diet (Chapter 6)

Listed below are some absolutely fantastic appetizer recipes for your enjoyment. Using the recipes that follow you may create them that are very tasty, healthful, and simple to prepare. Definitely going to check these out soon. Pancakes (Recipe No. 26).

Considering that pancakes are sugary, they are also illuminating; thus, give them to your family and friends and you will get rave praises.

Time Required for Preparation: 20 min 8 people can be accommodated with this recipe. Ingredients:

All-purpose flour (about 1 and a half cups). milk (one and one-fourth cups).

Egg (a single one).

3 and a half teaspoons of baking powder, if desired the salt (about 1 teaspoon).

the butter (about three tablespoons) (melted) sugar (white): 1 tablespoon

Directions:

Put all of the ingredients in a large mixing basin and whisk until well combined. This is a fantastic combination of words! Pour egg, milk, and butter into a well in the center of the cake.

In a smooth mixture, thoroughly combine the ingredients. coat the pan with olive oil before you start cooking in it Set the heat to medium. Pour the pancake batter onto the heated pan and cook it for half a minute, or until the edges are golden. Permit both sides of the meat to get a dark brown color. Use your favorite syrup or sauce to accompany it. The recipe for Recipe 27 is a snack made using almonds and chicken.

There is nothing missing from this nutritious and unique cuisine. It has the most fantastic texture as well as an incredible appearance.

Duration of Preparation: 55 min The following ingredients are used to feed four people.

The chicken thigh weighs 500 grams (without skin and bones) 3 medium red onions (slices of red onion) (thick wedges)

1 red potato (500 g) (thick slices)

3 medium-sized red peppers, seeded but not cut into slices 1 garlic clove, peeled and minced

cumin, fennel seeds, and smoked paprika (1 tsp. each) in a small mortar and pestle the equivalent of three tablespoons Olive oil is a kind of oil that comes from the olive fruit.

1 lemon (including the zest and juice) Blanched almonds, roughly chopped (50 grams) Recipe includes 170g of Greek yogurt as an ingredient. Fresh parsley in a little handful

Directions:

Oven preheating at 400 degrees Fahrenheit Put everything in a big mixing bowl and mix well. Season the chicken with the seasonings and mix well.

Mix together the spices, lemon juice and garlic in a separate basin before adding the oil, olive oil, and lemon zest. Bake in two baking plates once you've spread the mixture over the potatoes and the chicken.

Roast it in the oven for 40 minutes, and then cook it for another 20 minutes. Additionally, add almonds.

In a separate dish, combine them with one tablespoon of minced parsley and yogurt.

Directions:

Fry the onion for around 4 minutes in 2 tablespoons of olive oil. Maintain a low temperature. Now, combine the mustard and honey in a small bowl and set it aside until you need it.

Take a bowl and put it in your hands. Make four patties for a burger by combining all of the burger ingredients together. Put one tablespoon of olive oil in a skillet and fry the burger patties until they are browned on both sides, about five minutes. Cook them for 10-12 minutes, depending on their size. Honey and mustard sauce may be served on the side with any bread or bun of your choosing.

Burger patties may also be topped with a variety of ingredients such as mushrooms, honey mustard, tomato, sautéed tomato, and romaine lettuce.

CPSIA information can be obtained
at www.ICGtesting.com
Printed in the USA
LVHW060717090922
727942LV00007B/266